Images
of
North Carolina

First Printing October, 1991
Robert D. Shangle, Publisher

Library of Congress Cataloging-in-Publication Data
Images of North Carolina
p.   cm.   ISBN 1-55988-302-2 (soft bound): $6.95
1. North Carolina — Description and travel — 1981 — Views. I. LTA Publishing Company.
F255.I44 1991   917.5604'43 — dc20   91-23707—   CIP

Copyright © 1991 by LTA Publishing Company
Production, Concept and Distribution by LTA Publishing Company, Portland, Oregon.
Printed in Thailand. This book produced as the major component of the "World Peace and
Understanding" program of Beauty of America Printing Company, Portland, Oregon.

Introduction

"What a beautiful area!" "I want to remember this forever!" "It's absolutely awesome!" "The Creator simply out-did Himself!"

All of these statements are descriptive of the thoughts expressed when viewing this great State of North Carolina that we live in, work in, and play in. And why not. This is a Grand Place.

Images linger in our mind's eye, bringing back those memories of excitement, happiness, family, loved ones, places we've visited, or always dreamed of visiting. One can remember, either because "I've been there," or visited vicariously. We want to hold onto those experiences of "places I've been, things I've done, places I want to see."

The images in this book have been gathered together to assist with those memories and you can give it life. Combining these pictures with your memories make them fill with energy, telling your story that is full of excitement and thrills.

A tribute to North Carolina!

Orton Plantation Near Wilmington

Wright Brothers Memorial, Kitty Hawk

Smoky Mountain National Park

Along The Blue Ridge Parkway

Harker Island

Attic Window Peak, Grandfather Mountain

Bodie Island Lighthouse, Cape Hatteras

On Cape Hatteras

Indian Creek Falls, Great Smoky Mountain National Park

Tryon Palace in New Bern

Whitewater Falls

Somerset Place Historic Site

Grandfather Mountain

On Cape Hatteras

Farmland Along Blue Ridge Parkway Near Sparta

Guilford Courthouse National Military Park

Winter Snow in The Great Smoky Mountains

Orton Plantation Near Wilmington

Jolkey Ridge State Park

The Great Smoky Mountains From Mile High Overlook

Cape Hatteras Lighthouse

At Marshallburg

Near Jordan Lake

Linville Falls

Table Rock in The Blue Ridge Mountains

The Great Smoky Mountains From Mile High Overlook

Crabtree Falls

In Great Smoky Mountain National Park

The Henrietta II at Wilmington

Silver Lake on Ocracoke Island

Greenfield Gardens, Wilmington

Oregon Inlet Area, Cape Hatteras

Old Winston-Salem

Tom's Branch Falls, Great Smoky Mountain National Park

Elizabethan Gardens, Roanoke Island

At Cades Cove in The Great Smoky Mountains

Along The Blue Ridge Parkway

On Cape Hatteras

Near Cashiers

Pilots Knob (elevation 2,400 feet)

Salvo Beach, Cape Hatteras

Pioneer Homestead, Great Smoky Mountain National Park

Intracoastal Waterway, Morehead City

Biltmore Estate, Asheville

Along The Blue Ridge Parkway

Blue Valley, From The Top of Glen Falls

Pioneer Homestead In The Great Smoky Mountains

Nags Head, On The Outer Banks